A **TRUE** BOOK

The Oregon Trail

MEL FRIEDMAN

Children's Press®
An Imprint of Scholastic Inc.
New York Toronto London Auckland Sydney
Mexico City New Delhi Hong Kong
Danbury, Connecticut

Content Consultant
David R. Smith, Ph.D.
Adjunct Assistant Professor of History
University of Michigan
Ann Arbor, Michigan

Library of Congress Cataloging-in-Publication Data

Friedman, Mel, 1946–
  The Oregon Trail / by Mel Friedman.
     p. cm.—(A true book)
  Includes bibliographical references and index.
    ISBN-13: 978-0-531-20584-6 (lib. bdg.)   978-0-531-21247-9 (pbk.)
    ISBN-10: 0-531-20584-3 (lib. bdg.)   0-531-21247-5 (pbk.)

  1. Pioneers—Oregon National Historic Trail—History—9th
century—Juvenile literature. 2. Pioneers—Oregon National Historic
Trail—Social life and customs—19th century—Juvenile literature. 3.
Frontier and pioneer life—Oregon National Historic Trail—Juvenile
literature. 4. Overland journeys to the Pacific—Juvenile literature.
5. Oregon National Historic Trail—History—Juvenile literature. I.
Title. II. Series.

  F597.F75 2010
  978'.02—dc22   2009014186

All rights reserved. Published in 2010 by Children's Press, an imprint of Scholastic Inc.
Published simultaneously in Canada. Printed in China.
SCHOLASTIC, CHILDREN'S PRESS, A TRUE BOOK, and associated logos are trademarks and/or
registered trademarks of Scholastic Inc.

2 3 4 5 6 7 8 9 10 R 19 18 17 16 15 14 13 12 11 10   62

Find the Truth!

Everything you are about to read is true *except* for one of the sentences on this page.

Which one is **TRUE**?

T or F   Native Americans never helped the pioneers.

T or F   Railroads drew people away from the Oregon Trail.

Find the answers in this book.

3

Contents

THE **BIG** TRUTH!

The Man Who Saved the Trail

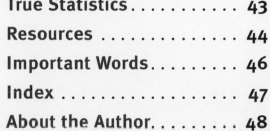

Wagon wheel tracks are visible today in many places along the Oregon Trail.

A modern-day wagon train re-creates part of the pioneers' trip along the Oregon Trail.

CHAPTER 1

A Great Adventure

On May 22, 1843, nearly 1,000 men, women, and children gathered in a campground for covered wagons near Independence, Missouri. Excitement was in the air. These brave Americans were called **pioneers**. They were about to begin a great adventure. Soon they would be setting out on a long journey west, with hopes of creating better lives for themselves.

The Oregon Trail crossed land that now makes up six U.S. states.

Hitting the Trail

The Oregon Trail was the most important pioneer route to the American West in the 1800s. Between 1830 and 1860, some 300,000 people followed the trail and its branches to Oregon, California, and other U.S. **territories** beyond the Rocky Mountains.

The solid black line shows the Oregon Trail's route west. Pioneers also used the other trails shown on this map.

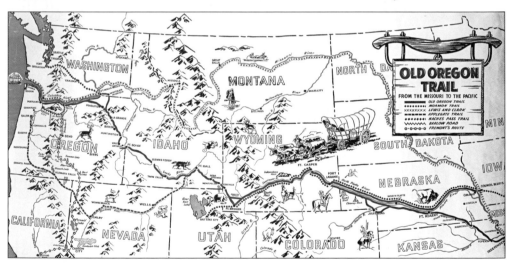

The Oregon Trail was 2,000 miles (3,200 kilometers) long!

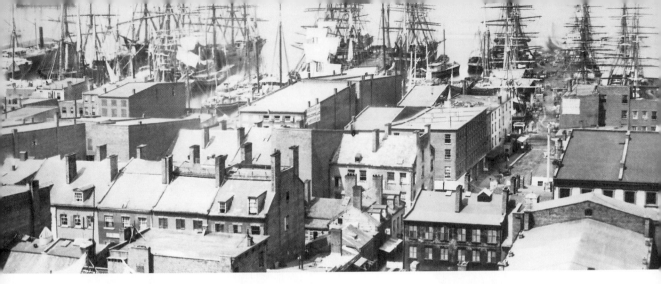

Overcrowded cities such as New York led pioneers to go west in search of more land.

Reasons for Leaving

Before pioneers began using the trail, most Americans lived on a narrow stretch of land along the East Coast. Once people began moving west, Americans spread farther across the **continent**.

The pioneers had different reasons for traveling west. Some were searching for more land or better places to farm. Others were trying to strike it rich. They all took great risks traveling through areas they knew little about.

CHAPTER 2

Claiming the West

The Oregon Trail started in western Missouri and ended in Oregon City, a pioneer town on the Pacific Coast of North America. The trail wound its way across **prairies**, dangerous rivers, high mountains, and hot deserts. In the early 1800s, before Americans started heading west, these lands were home to Native American tribes such as the Sioux (SOO), Blackfoot, Crow, and Shoshone (show-SHOW-nee).

Until the 1850s and 1860s, only Native Americans lived in what became the midwestern United States.

European Neighbors in the West

The United States was much smaller in 1800 than it is today. It had only 16 states plus a few territories. The country stopped at the Mississippi River. Beyond the river were small **colonies** controlled by France, Spain, Great Britain, and Russia. All of these countries were looking to control more land.

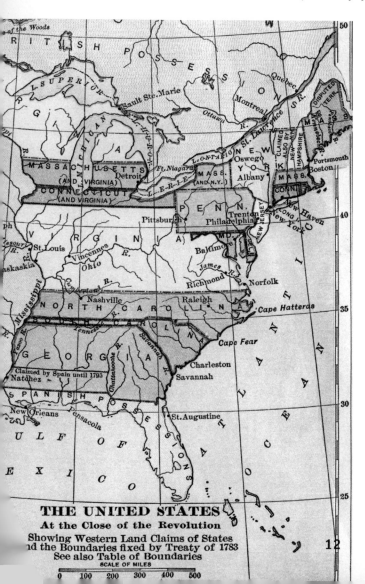

THE UNITED STATES
At the Close of the Revolution
Showing Western Land Claims of States
nd the Boundaries fixed by Treaty of 1783
See also Table of Boundaries
SCALE OF MILES
0   100   200   300   400   500

Heceta Head lighthouse is located near Florence, Oregon.

Heceta Head lighthouse, on the Oregon coast, was named for Bruno de Heceta.

The Search for a Great River

Early European explorers had heard stories of cities made of gold in North America. While searching for these cities, they stumbled on what became Oregon. The explorers also looked for a great river that was said to flow across North America, emptying into the Pacific Ocean. This river was known as the Northwest Passage. In 1775, Spanish explorer Bruno de Heceta (hay-SEE-tuh) was the first European to set foot in Oregon.

Oregon Country

In 1792, Robert Gray, an American ship captain, found and named Oregon's Columbia River. His voyage established America's earliest claim, or right to own land, in what would be called Oregon Country.

Oregon Country covered a huge area. It extended from the Pacific Ocean to the Rocky Mountains and from northern California to Alaska. It included present-day Oregon, Washington, and Idaho, and parts of Montana, Wyoming, and Canada.

Robert Gray (in blue coat) meets with Native Americans along the Oregon coast. Gray named the Columbia River after his ship.

Contest for Control

For decades, beaver furs were the most important item traded between Native Americans and Europeans.

Besides Spain, two other European nations were looking to expand their colonies in the Northwest. Russia controlled Alaska and traded fur as far south as San Francisco. Great Britain, also involved in the fur trade, was pushing into western Canada and had a strong claim to Oregon. By the early 1800s, a contest for control of Oregon was building between the United States and Great Britain.

 Once he went ashore, Captain Gray buried coins in the ground to prove that Americans had visited Oregon.

Lewis and Clark were helped by a Shoshone woman guide named Sacagawea (sak-uh-juh-WEE-uh).

CHAPTER 3

The Trail Opens

In 1803, U.S. president Thomas Jefferson bought the Louisiana Territory from France. The territory covered 828,800 square miles (2,147,000 square kilometers) of land. This famous deal, the Louisiana Purchase, doubled the amount of land controlled by the United States.

In 1804, Jefferson sent a team headed by captains Meriwether Lewis and William Clark to explore this territory and neighboring Oregon. Jefferson hoped they would find the Northwest Passage and help America gain more control over Oregon.

The "Brown Gold" Rush

In 1806, Lewis and Clark returned from their journey. They had not found the Northwest Passage, because it didn't exist. But their glowing reports of Oregon's rich soil and rivers filled with beavers soon sent trappers—people who caught animals for their furs—rushing west. At the time, beaver fur was in fashion, and traders could make lots of money selling it. They called the fur "brown gold."

Beaver pelts, or skins, like these were a common sight at fur-trading posts throughout the Northwest in the early 1800s.

At one time, a single beaver fur sold for about $30—one month's salary for the average worker!

Mountain men knew the way over rough terrain and through dangerous mountain passes.

A Pass Is Found

Fur trappers, known as mountain men, became the trail's next great explorers. The trail through the Rocky Mountains was one of the most difficult sections these men faced. In 1812, trapper Robert Stuart found a pass, or opening, through the Rockies that wagons could cross. However, a war with Great Britain had just broken out, so Americans slowed their travel west. Stuart's route was forgotten for years.

Wagons Start Rolling

In 1818, the United States and Great Britain agreed to share control of Oregon. At first, the only way American pioneers could reach Oregon was by ship. They sailed around the southern tip of South America and up the Pacific Coast. In 1824, two mountain men, Jedediah (je-duh-DYE-uh) Smith and Thomas Fitzpatrick, rediscovered Stuart's route, called South Pass. With that, the first pioneer wagons were rolling west along the Oregon Trail by 1832.

South Pass is located in what is now Wyoming.

Most Americans lived far from the ocean, so a sea voyage to Oregon was not possible. South Pass opened a land route to Oregon.

Rock Star

Early pioneers didn't have accurate maps, so they often used **landmarks** to guide them. The trail's most famous landmark was Chimney Rock in western Nebraska. It was a huge, reddish rock topped by a stone "chimney" that reached more than 300 feet (91 meters) high. Chimney Rock marked the end of the prairie and the beginning of the slow, steady climb toward the Rocky Mountains.

Chimney Rock could be seen from 40 mi. (64 km) away!

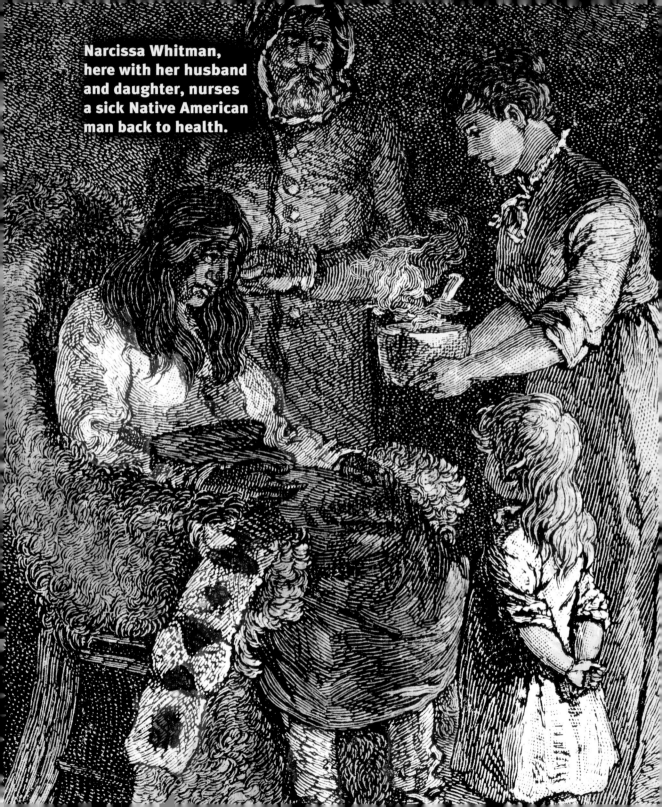

Narcissa Whitman, here with her husband and daughter, nurses a sick Native American man back to health.

CHAPTER 4

Hopes and Dreams

The first settlers to take wagons to Oregon were **missionaries**. They went there to convert Native Americans to Christianity. In 1836, missionaries Narcissa Whitman and Eliza Spalding became the first pioneer women to cross the Rocky Mountains with their husbands. They proved that women as well as men could survive on the trail. Families back East believed that they, too, could handle the journey.

 Narcissa Whitman became a missionary at age 16.

"Oregon Fever"

In the 1840s, wonderful descriptions of Oregon, written by missionaries and mountain men, began to appear in newspapers and books. Many Americans dreamed of starting farms and businesses in Oregon. Others talked of moving to Oregon to drive out the British. These people believed that America had a right to expand from the Atlantic Ocean to the Pacific Ocean. This belief was known as **Manifest Destiny**.

This booklet was written to encourage people to come to Oregon. It describes the land of the Oregon Territory and what life there was like for settlers.

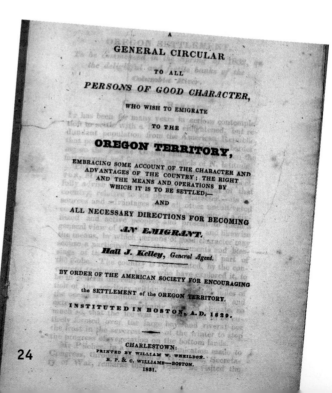

A

GENERAL CIRCULAR

TO ALL

PERSONS OF GOOD CHARACTER,

WHO WISH TO EMIGRATE

TO THE

OREGON TERRITORY,

EMBRACING SOME ACCOUNT OF THE CHARACTER AND ADVANTAGES OF THE COUNTRY; THE RIGHT AND THE MEANS AND OPERATIONS BY WHICH IT IS TO BE SETTLED;—

AND

ALL NECESSARY DIRECTIONS FOR BECOMING

AN EMIGRANT.

Hall J. Kelley, General Agent.

BY ORDER OF THE AMERICAN SOCIETY FOR ENCOURAGING

the SETTLEMENT of the OREGON TERRITORY.

INSTITUTED IN BOSTON, A.D. 1829.

CHARLESTOWN:
PRINTED BY WILLIAM W. WHEILDON.
R. P. & C. WILLIAMS—BOSTON.
1831.

The California gold rush caused people to need lumber and other items. In 1850, Oregon became a source for these things, and people who sold what the miners needed became wealthy.

Searching for Gold

In 1846, journalist Horace Greeley urged adventurous men to follow their dreams to the new **frontier**. "Go west, young man, go west!" he wrote. By the 1850s, tens of thousands of Americans had done just that. Traffic along the Oregon Trail had increased. Gold had been discovered in California in 1848. Thousands of travelers were following the trail's southern branch to the California goldfields.

The Man Who Saved the Trail

Ezra Meeker first journeyed to Oregon in 1852. Later in life, he worried that Americans had forgotten the Oregon Trail. So in 1906, at the age of 76, he decided to take his journey again in an ox-drawn covered wagon, this time going east.

Along the way, Meeker urged people to save the trail. His efforts led directly to the trail's protection by the U.S. government.

In 1924, at the age of 94, Meeker flew over the trail by airplane from Washington State to Ohio.

The pioneers packed wagons with seeds, farming tools, saws, blankets, clothes, lanterns, mirrors, paper, pens, and medicines.

A fully loaded covered wagon could weigh as much as 2,000 pounds (907 kilograms).

A Long Walk

Life on the trail was hard. Wagons weren't large enough to store all of the pioneers' belongings. So everyone except for young children, the old, the ill, and pregnant women walked the entire way. This was usually a 2,000-mi. (3,200 km) journey that took between four and six months. Every evening, wagons had to be unloaded for dinner and sleeping. Every morning, they were reloaded for the day's hike.

Home Sweet Wagon

The typical wagon was narrow, so it could fit between the rock walls of mountain passes. Wagons were also sturdy enough to take the bumpy ride. They had wooden wheels wrapped with iron bands, a hand brake, and a canvas cover for protection from rain and dust. Wagons were pulled by teams of oxen or mules. Families slept in their wagons or in tents.

The Daily Routine

Pioneers awoke at sunrise. They gave their animals food and water, repaired the wagons, and ate breakfasts of coffee, bacon, and dry bread. Then they walked the trail, with a short break for lunch. Just before sundown, they set up camp. In the evening, parents taught their children, and many pioneers joined in singing, dancing, and storytelling around the campfire.

Sights on the Trail

Travelers observed many strange and wonderful things on the trail. They saw wildflowers blooming, bison roaming, and prairie dogs popping out of holes in the ground. But travelers also passed sad sights such as the graves of pioneers who had died. The trail was also littered with personal belongings that pioneers were forced to leave behind to lighten their wagons.

Bison were known as the kings of the plains.

With few trees on the trail, pioneers often burned bison droppings, called buffalo chips, in place of firewood.

CHAPTER 5

Challenges along the Way

Stories of dangers along the trail traveled with the pioneers. Although pioneers worried about Native American attacks, such attacks didn't happen often. Since the time of Lewis and Clark's journey, Native Americans had helped the pioneers they met. They shared what they knew about the trail, traded with the pioneers, helped them find food and water, and guided some wagon trains west.

Native Americans often visited pioneer camps to sell the travelers dried meat, fish, or vegetables.

Mountain Friend

Moses "Black" Harris was an African American mountain man who was born into slavery. Once he gained his freedom, he worked as a trapper, trader, and wagon train guide. Strong, tough and fearless, he helped build Fort Laramie in Wyoming, a stopping point on the Oregon Trail. He twice rescued lost wagon trains. He was a friend to Native Americans and spoke several Indian languages. He died of a disease called cholera (KOL-er-uh) in 1849.

Moses "Black" Harris (left) was one of the best known mountain men. He was a friend to pioneers and Native Americans.

Only about half of the original 87 members of the Donner-Reed group survived.

The Donner-Reed group's wagons and animals were buried under 40-foot (12-meter) drifts of snow.

Tragedy in the Mountains

Pioneers who didn't make it past the western mountains before autumn—when snow usually began to fall—risked disaster. In October 1846, the Donner-Reed wagon train became trapped in the mountains by a huge snowstorm. Food ran out, and people began dying. Some went for help. The starving pioneers who were left behind survived by cooking and eating their dead friends. Eventually, the survivors were rescued.

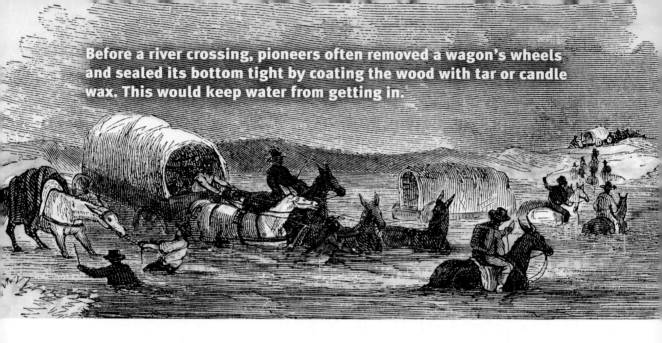

Before a river crossing, pioneers often removed a wagon's wheels and sealed its bottom tight by coating the wood with tar or candle wax. This would keep water from getting in.

Crossing Rivers

On the journey west, pioneers had to cross many rivers with their wagons and animals. River crossings could be dangerous.

If a river was shallow, wagons had to be pulled across by animal teams. If it was deep, wagons were floated across like boats, or carried. Sometimes pioneers or their animals drowned in swift currents or were sucked under by **quicksand** on the river bottom.

The Biggest Killer

Many pioneers were killed or injured in wagon accidents. But the biggest dangers by far were **infectious** diseases such as cholera, smallpox, scarlet fever, and influenza (in-floo-EN-zuh). Cholera, a sickness commonly caused by drinking unclean water, was the single biggest killer on the trail. Death usually occurred within 24 hours.

This grave near Sun Ranch, Wyoming, is believed to belong to a pioneer named T. P. Baker, thought to have died along the trail in 1864.

Mount Hood is one of Oregon's most well-known sights.

CHAPTER 6

The End of the Trail

In 1846, the United States and Great Britain
settled their dispute over control of Oregon.
Britain got the land north of the 49th **parallel**.
The United States got the land to the south.
Oregon became a U.S. territory in 1848. In 1859,
it became the 33rd U.S. state.

The beaver is Oregon's
state animal.

This is a view of San Francisco, California, around 1849.

Rail Versus Trail

Before the California gold rush, most pioneers were bound for Oregon. During the gold rush, traffic to Oregon slowed as many pioneers took the trail's southern branch to California. Even though pioneers were no longer traveling through Oregon, the state continued to grow.

Oregon Trail Timeline

1775

Explorer Bruno de Heceta arrives in Oregon.

1843

Many groups of pioneers begin traveling along the Oregon Trail.

The completion of the country's first transcontinental railroad drew people away from the Oregon Trail.

After 1869, the trail was no longer the best or fastest way to move west. Now people could travel by train. The transcontinental railroad became the first coast-to-coast railroad in the United States. People who could not afford a train ticket continued to use the Oregon Trail into the early 1900s, but its golden age was over.

1859
Oregon becomes the 33rd U.S. state.

1848
The California gold rush begins.

STATE OF OREGON

THE UNION

1859

Many pioneers carved their names into this landmark boulder, located in central Wyoming. Mountain men first came upon it on July 4, 1824, so they named it Independence Rock.

Independence Rock is 130 ft (40 m) high!

Now Part of History

Today, the Oregon Trail is a National Historic Trail, which means it is protected by the U.S. government. Sites such as Independence Rock and South Pass are now public parks or monuments. The brave people who traveled the Oregon Trail set out to build new lives. In doing so, they helped write the history of westward expansion in the United States. ★

True Statistics

Area of land gained by the Louisiana Purchase: 828,800 sq. mi. (2,147,000 sq. km)

Number of pioneers taking the trail in 1840: 13

Number of pioneers taking the trail in 1852: 10,000

Number of pioneers who died on the trail: Between 20,000 and 30,000

Distance a pioneer walked on an average day: About 15 to 20 mi. (24 to 32 km)

Average cost of buying a wagon and supplies for the trip west: About $1,500 (which equaled two years' salary for the average worker at this time)

Typical age range of pioneers: Between 16 and 35 years old

OLD
OREGON
TRAIL.
1843-57

Did you find the truth?

F Native Americans never helped the pioneers.

T Railroads drew people away from the Oregon Trail.

Resources

Books

Blackwood, Gary L. *Life on the Oregon Trail*. San Diego: Lucent Books, 1999.

Calabro, Marian. *The Perilous Journey of the Donner Party*. New York: Clarion, 1999.

Duncan, Dayton. *People of the West*. Boston: Little, Brown, 1996.

Emsden, Katharine. *Voices from the West: Life along the Trail*. Carlisle, MA: Discovery Enterprises, 1999.

Erickson, Paul. *Daily Life in a Covered Wagon*. New York: Puffin, 1997.

Hermes, Patricia. *Westward to Home: Joshua's Oregon Trail Diary*. New York: Scholastic, 2001.

Levine, Ellen, and Elroy Freem. *If You Traveled West in a Covered Wagon*. New York: Scholastic, 1992.

Manheimer, Ann S. *James Beckwourth: Legendary Mountain Man*. Minneapolis: Twenty-First Century Books, 2005.

Nelson, Sharlene, and Ted Nelson. *Jedediah Smith*. New York: Franklin Watts, 2004.

Palmer, Rosemary G. *Jim Bridger: Trapper, Trader, and Guide*. Mankato, Minnesota: Compass Point Books, 2007.

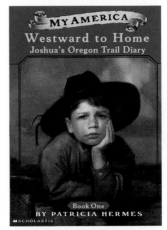

Organizations and Web Sites

End of the Oregon Trail Interpretive Center

www.historicoregoncity.org/HOC/index.php?option=com_content&view=category&id=75&Itemid=80

See how early settlers worked and lived in Oregon Country.

Fantastic Facts about the Oregon Trail

www.isu.edu/~trinmich/Facts.htm

Find out about weird covered wagons and a cow that started a war.

The Oregon Trail

www.historyglobe.com/ot/otmap1.html

Visit this site to see an interactive map describing landmarks of the trail.

Places to Visit

Meeker Mansion

312 Spring Street
Puyallup, WA 98372
(253) 848-1770
www.meekermansion.org/history.html
Visit the home of Ezra Meeker.

National Frontier Trails Museum

318 West Pacific
Independence, MO 64050
(816) 325-7575
www.ci.independence.mo.us/NFTM/
This museum and library are devoted to the history of America's western trails.

Important Words

colonies – areas ruled by other countries

continent – one of the seven large landmasses of the earth. The United States is located on the North American continent.

frontier – a border between a settled area and wild or unknown land

infectious – capable of causing a disease that can pass easily from person to person

landmarks – land features that serve as guides to travelers

Manifest Destiny – a belief in the 1800s that America had a right to expand across the continent

missionaries – people who try to spread their religious beliefs to others

parallel – any of the imaginary lines that circle the earth in the same direction as the equator

pioneers – people who are the first to move to or settle new areas

prairies – large areas of land with no trees but covered with grass

quicksand – watery sand that can pull down heavy objects

territories – lands owned or claimed by a country

Index

Page numbers in **bold** indicate illustrations

About the Author

Mel Friedman is an award-winning journalist and children's book author. He has four graduate degrees from Columbia University, including one in East Asian studies. He also holds a bachelor's degree in history from Lafayette College. Friedman has written or cowritten more than two dozen children's books, both fiction and nonfiction. He and his wife and their daughter often rescue stray dogs.